Joel

Obadiah

K.W. Bow

Copyright 2017 by Kenneth W. Bow
The book author retains sole copyright to
his contributions to this book.
Published 2017.
Printed in the United States of America.

All rights reserved.

No portion of this book may be reproduced, stored in a retrieval system, or transmitted in any form or by any means – electronic, mechanical, photocopy, recording, scanning, or other – except for brief quotations in critical reviews or articles, without the prior written permission of the author.

ISBN 978-1-946234-08-7

Front cover design by Mark Gauthier.

This book was published by BookCrafters,
Parker, Colorado.
bookcrafterscolorado@gmail.com

This book may be ordered from
www.bookcrafters.net and other online bookstores.

Foreword

Thank you reader, for selecting my book. There are many choices of books and we all have a limited window of time to read. I appreciate you purchasing my product. It is a humbling thing to know someone would choose to purchase, and then read your work. I do not take it as a small matter. By purchasing and reading a book, the reader and the author form a certain bond as they travel a road together for a short time. It is especially rewarding when the two agree on the content. It is my hope you can find inspiration and life challenges in the pages of this small booklet.

From the days of my high school years I have found the Bible fascinating. I have travelled to Israel on two occasions to learn more about the land and culture of the Bible. I worked on an archaeological dig and lived on a Kibbutz to better inform myself of how to understand this book from God. I have read it from cover to cover over twenty times, and it is still as exciting to me as it ever was.

The Bible is a magnificent journey and experience. It is ever a delight. In it you will travel to distant lands and meet some of the most incredible people of history. It will introduce you to kings and peasants. You will walk the palace halls of castles and the open fields of the countryside. You will meet the famous and be introduced to people whose name we will never know. You will read some of the greatest love stories ever told and you will see the dark side of man as the evil manifests itself in heinous ways. Every emotion of man is highlighted at some time. You will see greed and avarice and murderous covetousness. You will also see the greatest examples of love and sacrifice that mankind has ever contributed. For indeed the Bible is the story of man. It is the whole story, and nothing is left out or omitted. It is the ultimate mirror of life.

When we invest time in the Bible we indulge a bit of the eternal. The Bible will never pass away, even in the eons of the future. If you have read it sincerely then my hope is this small work will intensify your understanding and enjoyment a little more. It is the grandest journey we can make while in this life. Thank you for sharing a portion of your life journey with me.

Kenneth Bow

Joel

Introduction

Is a natural disaster an act of God? When earthquakes strike, or famines continue, are these the acts of God or are they just the result of life on planet earth? This Theist verses Deist argument has been around for 2500 years. Plato and his school discussed this ad infinitum. The prophet Joel had no hesitation. He boldly proclaimed this was God working among men.

The book of Joel is about a locust invasion. A swarm of locusts that covered the land and destroyed everything in sight. Joel's vision was God leading these locusts into battle like a general leads his troops (2.11). Joel encouraged the priests to call a national day of prayer and fasting to lead the people back to God. He promised if the people would return to God they would eat in plenty (2.26). Joel proposed this disaster could bring a backslidden nation back to God.

It was an uphill task for God's prophet. Joel's vision was that God's people would love God all the time, not just in times of disaster. It is human nature to turn to God in times of great tragedy. This book is an eternal appeal to all mankind to love God in the times of prosperity, and in the times of dearth.

It begins with the plague of locusts, and moves to the call for repentance. The day of the Lord is coming and the prophet is calling for men to turn back to God. One of the greatest promises of the Bible is in this small book. It is the promise of the coming Spirit of God being poured out on all flesh. This would happen centuries in the future on the day of Pentecost in Acts chapter 2. The prophecy then moves on to the judgment of Judah's enemies and the future eternal blessings on God's people.

This small book of three chapters covers some of the most profound questions mankind has asked throughout history. The conclusion is succinct and powerful. Whether it's a swarm of locusts, or nuclear war, God is in control. Turn to God and your future will be blessed and secure.

Chapter 1

1.1-3 The word of the Lord that came to Joel the son of Pethuel. 2 Hear this, ye old men, and give ear, all ye inhabitants of the land. Hath this been in your days, or even in the days of your fathers? 3 Tell ye your children of it, and let your children tell their children, and their children another generation.

1.1-3 The prophet gives his ancestry as the son of Pethuel, which means enlarged of God. He calls to the aged among the people to see if anyone remembers such a plague as they now experience? He encourages them to not let this moment be forgotten in the generations to come.

1.4-12 That which the palmerworm hath left hath the locust eaten; and that which the locust hath left hath the cankerworm eaten; and that which the cankerworm hath left hath the caterpiller eaten. 5 Awake, ye drunkards, and weep; and howl, all ye drinkers of wine, because of the new wine; for it is cut off from your mouth. 6 For a nation is come up upon my land, strong, and without number, whose teeth are the teeth of a lion, and he hath the cheek teeth of a great lion. 7 He hath laid my vine waste, and barked my fig tree: he hath made it clean bare, and cast it away; the branches thereof are made white. 8 Lament like a virgin girded with sackcloth for the husband of her youth. 9 The meat offering and the drink offering is cut off from the house of the Lord; the priests, the Lord's ministers, mourn. 10 The field is wasted, the land mourneth; for the corn is wasted: the new wine is dried up, the oil languisheth. 11 Be ye ashamed, O ye husbandmen; howl, O ye vinedressers, for the wheat and for the barley; because the harvest of the field is perished. 12 The vine is dried up, and the fig tree languisheth; the pomegranate tree, the palm tree also, and the apple tree, even all the trees of the field, are withered: because joy is withered away from the sons of men.

1.4-12 The devastation is documented. The terms of four destroying insects are offered. These are the palmerworm, the locust, the cankerworm and the caterpillar. These also represent the stages of the plague and the results. First there was a worm, then a grown locust that left behind eggs that would hatch again and bring yet another plague of young locusts. This vivid imagery was poignant to farmers for all future crops were in jeopardy. They would no sooner get one crop grown before the eggs gave birth to new young hordes of locusts and the cycle repeated itself again. The cycle would never end. This was the story of the people of God over the last six hundred years of Israel's history. The image of revolving failure was stark for the people to see. The total loss of meats, fig trees, corn, wine, wheat and barley, and pomegranates reflect the loss of joy in the hearts of the populace. They were facing a hopeless future.

1.13-20 Gird yourselves, and lament, ye priests: howl, ye ministers of the altar: come, lie all night in sackcloth, ye ministers of my God: for the meat offering and the drink offering is withholden from the house of your God. 14 Sanctify ye a fast, call a solemn assembly, gather the elders and all the inhabitants of the land into the house of the Lord your God, and cry unto the Lord, 15 Alas for the day! for the day of the Lord is at hand, and as a destruction from the Almighty shall it come. 16 Is not the meat cut off before our eyes, yea, joy and gladness from the house of our God? 17 The seed is rotten under their clods, the garners are laid desolate, the barns are broken down; for the corn is withered. 18 How do the beasts groan! the herds of cattle are perplexed, because they have no pasture; yea, the flocks of sheep are made desolate. 19 O Lord, to thee will I cry: for the fire hath devoured the pastures of the wilderness, and the flame hath burned all the trees of the field. 20 The beasts of the field cry also unto thee: for the rivers of waters are dried up, and the fire hath devoured the pastures of the wilderness.

1.13-20 The prophet starts with the answer; the priests. Joel calls the ministry to lament and howl and fast. The hunger is a result of the spiritual famine and leaving God. The natural disaster is a mirror of what has happened to the nation spiritually. The seed is rotten, the barns are broken down, and the beasts have no pasture. The future is bleak unless the people turn back to their God.

Chapter 2

2.1-2 Blow ye the trumpet in Zion, and sound an alarm in my holy mountain: let all the inhabitants of the land tremble: for the day of the Lord cometh, for it is nigh at hand; 2 A day of darkness and of gloominess, a day of clouds and of thick darkness, as the morning spread upon the mountains: a great people and a strong; there hath not been ever the like, neither shall be any more after it, even to the years of many generations.

2.1-2 The trumpet. The sounding of the trumpet was a call to religious gathering. Here the prophet uses the metaphor to signal God is sounding a trumpet. This will be repeated in the New Testament by Paul and John the revelator in the books of 1 Corinthians and Revelation.

2.3-11 A fire devoureth before them; and behind them a flame burneth: the land is as the garden of Eden before them, and behind them a desolate wilderness; yea, and nothing shall escape them. 4 The appearance of them is as the appearance of horses; and as horsemen, so shall they run. 5 Like the noise of chariots on the tops of mountains shall they leap, like the noise of a flame of fire that devoureth the stubble, as a strong people set in battle array. 6 Before their face the people shall be

much pained: all faces shall gather blackness. 7 They shall run like mighty men; they shall climb the wall like men of war; and they shall march every one on his ways, and they shall not break their ranks: 8 Neither shall one thrust another; they shall walk every one in his path: and when they fall upon the sword, they shall not be wounded. 9 They shall run to and fro in the city; they shall run upon the wall, they shall climb up upon the houses; they shall enter in at the windows like a thief. 10 The earth shall quake before them; the heavens shall tremble: the sun and the moon shall be dark, and the stars shall withdraw their shining: 11 And the Lord shall utter his voice before his army: for his camp is very great: for he is strong that executeth his word: for the day of the Lord is great and very terrible; and who can abide it?

2.3-11 The day of the Lord. This is a major theme of the Old Testament. Joel is sounding the alarm that the day is approaching rapidly. Joel likens it to a scorched earth scenario. This is common among the peoples of that day. Armies many times used this technique to render an opponent helpless. In the case of God it is a reflection of the completeness of His anger and judgment. The analogy of locusts is to chariots and warhorses. The destruction will be complete. The day of the Lord will be terrible and who can abide it?

2.12-17 Therefore also now, saith the Lord, turn ye even to me with all your heart, and with fasting, and with weeping, and with mourning: 13 And rend your heart, and not your garments, and turn unto the Lord your God: for he is gracious and merciful, slow to anger, and of great kindness, and repenteth him of the evil. 14 Who knoweth if he will return and repent, and leave a blessing behind him; even a meat offering and a drink offering unto the Lord your God? 15 Blow the trumpet in Zion, sanctify a fast, call a solemn assembly: 16 Gather the people, sanctify the congregation, assemble the elders, gather the children, and those that suck the breasts: let the bridegroom go forth of his chamber, and the bride out of her closet. 17 Let the priests, the ministers of the Lord, weep between the porch and the altar, and let them say, Spare thy people, O Lord, and give not thine heritage to reproach, that the heathen should rule over them: wherefore should they say among the people, Where is their God?

2.12-17 The appeal to return. It is not too late. God is still reaching for His people. Turn to the Lord with weeping and mourning. God is slow to anger and merciful. Begin with the priests and a call to repentance. This is the second time Joel metaphorically sounds the trumpet.

2.18-27 Then will the Lord be jealous for his land, and pity his people. 19 Yea, the Lord will answer and say unto his people, Behold, I will send you corn, and wine, and oil, and ye shall be satisfied therewith: and I will no more make you a reproach among the heathen: 20 But I will remove far off from you the northern army, and will drive him into a land barren and desolate, with his face toward the east sea, and his hinder part toward the utmost sea, and his stink shall come up, and his ill savour shall come up, because he hath done great things. 21 Fear not, O land; be glad and rejoice: for the Lord will do great things. 22 Be not afraid, ye beasts of the field: for the pastures of the wilderness do spring, for the tree beareth her fruit, the fig tree and the vine do yield their strength. 23 Be glad then, ye children of Zion, and rejoice in the Lord your God: for he hath given you the former rain moderately, and he will cause to come down for you the rain, the former rain, and the latter rain in the first month. 24 And the floors shall be full of wheat, and the vats shall overflow with wine and oil. 25 And I will restore to you the years that the locust hath eaten, the cankerworm, and the caterpiller, and the palmerworm, my great army which I sent among you. 26 And ye shall eat in plenty, and be satisfied, and praise the name of the Lord your God, that hath dealt wondrously with you: and my people shall never be ashamed. 27 And ye shall know that I am in the midst of Israel, and that I am the Lord your God, and none else: and my people shall never be ashamed.

2.18-27 The beauty of God's judgment is it did not last forever. It was for a season. The prophet now shifts his eye to the restoration of the people of God. There will be restoration of the very things the locust destroyed. Wheat, corn, wine, oil, and all the beasts of the field will again be plentiful. The fruit trees will again bear in their season. The promise is to restore everything taken away by the locusts. The prophet now moves into the great prophecy of the coming of the Spirit of God fulfilled in Acts chapter 2.

2.28-32 And it shall come to pass afterward, that I will pour out my spirit upon all flesh; and your sons and your daughters shall prophesy, your old men shall dream dreams, your young men shall see visions: 29 And also upon the servants and upon the handmaids in those days will I pour out my spirit. 30 And I will shew wonders in the heavens and in the earth, blood, and fire, and pillars of smoke. 31 The sun shall be turned into darkness, and the moon into blood, before the great and terrible day of the Lord come. 32 And it shall come to pass, that whosoever shall call on the name of the Lord shall be

delivered: for in mount Zion and in Jerusalem shall be deliverance, as the Lord hath said, and in the remnant whom the Lord shall call.

2.28-32 This prophecy is one of the turning points of the Old Testament and points to the great outpouring of the Holy Ghost in Acts 2. God reveals His will to indwell every person who will allow Him to live inside them. In the bigger picture of planet earth, the destruction caused by the fall of Adam and Eve will be restored by the spiritual rain that falls in Acts chapter 2. This is the restoration God has provided for all of mankind. Mankind was destroyed by sin in the garden and now God has provided complete restoration through His in dwelling spirit. All things destroyed by the fall are now restored in Jesus Christ. Peter confirms this when he preaches the first message of the New Testament era in Acts 2. Peter quotes this passage as proof of God's spirit indwelling believers. The moment in Acts 2, when the Holy Ghost falls is the pinnacle of all God's purpose and promise to humankind. From that moment, the eternal purpose of God is made manifest; God came to earth to save all of mankind.

Chapter 3

3.1-8 For, behold, in those days, and in that time, when I shall bring again the captivity of Judah and Jerusalem, 2 I will also gather all nations, and will bring them down into the valley of Jehoshaphat, and will plead with them there for my people and for my heritage Israel, whom they have scattered among the nations, and parted my land. 3 And they have cast lots for my people; and have given a boy for an harlot, and sold a girl for wine, that they might drink. 4 Yea, and what have ye to do with me, O Tyre, and Zidon, and all the coasts of Palestine? will ye render me a recompence? and if ye recompense me, swiftly and speedily will I return your recompence upon your own head; 5 Because ye have taken my silver and my gold, and have carried into your temples my goodly pleasant things: 6 The children also of Judah and the children of Jerusalem have ye sold unto the Grecians, that ye might remove them far from their border. 7 Behold, I will raise them out of the place whither ye have sold them, and will return your recompence upon your own head: 8 And I will sell your sons and your daughters into the hand of the children of Judah, and they shall sell them to the Sabeans, to a people far off: for the Lord hath spoken it.

3.1-8 The prophet extends the eye of prophecy to all the nations of the world. There will be a gathering of all nations into the valley of Jehoshaphat. This is referring to the great battle of Armageddon in the future. The battle of Armageddon will balance the scales of all the wrongs listed in these verses by the nations that opposed God.

3.9-16 Proclaim ye this among the Gentiles; Prepare war, wake up the mighty men, let all the men of war draw near; let them come up: 10 Beat your plowshares into swords and your pruninghooks into spears: let the weak say, I am strong. 11 Assemble yourselves, and come, all ye heathen, and gather yourselves together round about: thither cause thy mighty ones to come down, O Lord. 12 Let the heathen be wakened, and come up to the valley of Jehoshaphat: for there will I sit to judge all the heathen round about. 13 Put ye in the sickle, for the harvest is ripe: come, get you down; for the press is full, the fats overflow; for their wickedness is great. 14 Multitudes, multitudes in the valley of decision: for the day of the Lord is near in the valley of decision. 15 The sun and the moon shall be darkened, and the stars shall withdraw their shining. 16 The Lord also shall roar out of Zion, and utter his voice from Jerusalem; and the heavens and the earth shall shake: but the Lord will be the hope of his people, and the strength of the children of Israel.

3.9-16 The greatest battle of all history is now spoken of. The Gentile nations are awakened. Plowshares are beaten into instruments of war, and pruning hooks into spears. This is the great harvest of the ages in which God will bring mankind to answer for his rebellion. There will be reactions from nature in the sun and the moon. The stars will go black. God will roar out of heaven and proclaim

His rightful place as King of Kings and Lord of Lords. This is the ultimate war of good verses evil, and good triumphs forever.

3.17-21 So shall ye know that I am the Lord your God dwelling in Zion, my holy mountain: then shall Jerusalem be holy, and there shall no strangers pass through her any more. 18 And it shall come to pass in that day, that the mountains shall drop down new wine, and the hills shall flow with milk, and all the rivers of Judah shall flow with waters, and a fountain shall come forth out of the house of the Lord, and shall water the valley of Shittim. 19 Egypt shall be a desolation, and Edom shall be a desolate wilderness, for the violence against the children of Judah, because they have shed innocent blood in their land. 20 But Judah shall dwell for ever, and Jerusalem from generation to generation. 21 For I will cleanse their blood that I have not cleansed: for the Lord dwelleth in Zion.

3.17-21 The aftermath of war. God will restore earth and He himself will rule as King. Earth rejoices with plentiful crops and abundance. Jerusalem takes her rightful place as the capitol of the world. In these final sweeping verses, Joel captures the promise of the ages of almighty God to His faithful followers. The devastation at their feet left from the invasion of locusts that represent judgment, will give way to the glorious morning of Christ's rule on Earth. All things will be restored and God shall fill all in all.

Obadiah

Introduction

This book, like others in sacred canon, is sometimes looked at and pondered. It would be more plausible if it contained world views or clashing armies with world changing moments. Instead it is about a feud between two brothers that spans hundreds of years. So the question arises, why is this in the Bible? What eternal truth was so valuable that God said every generation needs to read this and adjust their life to be saved? The Bible is our roadmap to get to heaven and each book and chapter serves that purpose in some manner. So how does the story of twin brothers in a life long feud serve millenniums of pilgrims headed for a celestial city?

To add to the mystic, the author is anonymous. There is no certainty who he is for sure. Then add to the conundrum the date of the writing. It is also uncertain. We are left with the simple concept that God felt this scroll was important. This book is an important detail to the overall body of the Bible. It is the shortest book in the Bible. The author can be anyone from a King's courier and temple confidant, to an unknown person. The message God is sending seems to be, focus on the content, not the container.

These twins, Jacob and Esau, struggled in their mother's

womb. Even in their birth there was conflict with Jacob holding his brother's heel. Throughout their life this open conflict continued. The details are recorded in the sacred canon. This book details how God views such issues. In the larger span of life, this conflict speaks to universal man. Life is a conflict. How we react and interact with that conflict determines not only our eternal salvation, but also our quality of life. The depth of the Bible is ever about layers of truth. Never more so than in this brief interlude in your daily reading. How you react to your brother is important to God. God documents your secret thoughts and all your insidious motives. This is the far reaching meaning of this smallest of books. God watches if you rejoice when your brother struggles. God is documenting the moment if you assist in your brother's demise. Just as God wrote down the motives and machinations of Esau and his lineage, He is documenting ours as well. The resounding echo of this small compendium is that we live carefully and cognizant of this. Jesus emphatically stated, Thou shalt love thy neighbor as thyself.

Chapter 1

1.1-3 The vision of Obadiah. Thus saith the Lord God concerning Edom; We have heard a rumour from the Lord, and an ambassador is sent among the heathen, Arise ye, and let us rise up against her in battle. 2 Behold, I have made thee small among the heathen: thou art greatly despised. 3 The pride of thine heart hath deceived thee, thou that dwellest in the clefts of the rock, whose habitation is high; that saith in his heart, Who shall bring me down to the ground?

1.1-3 We are not privy to know which Obadiah in the scripture this is, or if he is any of those listed in the Bible. The importance here is not the messenger, but rather the message. God does not leave out or hide details to be evasive. God chooses to put in the details He sees necessary. The issue is concerning Edom, the lineage of Esau. As Edom rises to battle against his brother Israel, God rises to battle against Edom. God made Edom small and despised. God exposed the pride of Edom's heart to the world. God pulled away Edom's bogus safety of the high craggy cliffs of Petra. Edom has ascended not only the rocky heights of Petra, but like Lucifer he climbed the heights of pride. This pinnacle will always cause a fall.

1.4-6 Though thou exalt thyself as the eagle, and though thou set thy nest among the stars, thence will I bring thee down, saith the Lord. 5 If thieves came to thee, if robbers by night, (how art thou cut off!) would they not have stolen till they had enough? if the grapegatherers came to thee, would they not leave some grapes? 6 How are the things of Esau searched out! how are his hidden things sought up!

1.4-6 By man's standard Esau's descendants were very high and secure. By God's standard, they were just another foolish pride to be cast down. The almighty lets them know his battle with them will leave no prisoners and give no quarter. Thieves or robbers would not utterly destroy, they would only take the valuables. God needs no valuables. God is not there to plunder. If men were gathering grapes, they would leave some behind. God has no such intentions. God has tolerated this feud for generations and now the judgment falls. One of the most poetic and focused moments in scripture is penned by an unknown author in an unknown time. "How are the things of Esau searched out?" The original language speaks of secret things. This goes far beyond visible things. Esau is about to be removed forever. The only thing left will be a vague memory of a once proud people.

1.7-9 All the men of thy confederacy have brought thee even to the border: the men that were at peace with thee have deceived thee, and prevailed against thee; they that eat thy bread have laid a wound under thee: there is none understanding in him. 8 Shall I not in that day, saith the Lord, even destroy the wise men out of Edom, and understanding out of the mount of Esau? 9 And thy mighty men, O Teman, shall be dismayed, to the end

that every one of the mount of Esau may be cut off by slaughter.

1.7-9 The striping of Edom will include his confederates. Those he sought laughter and solace in will now oppose him and Edom will feel the lash of their derision. Edom is now going to feel the stab in the back he has subjected Jacob to. Jesus confirmed this in His teaching, "with what judgment ye judge, ye shall be judged". The wise and mighty men of Edom are now cut off by slaughter and a violent death.

1.10-14 For thy violence against thy brother Jacob shame shall cover thee, and thou shalt be cut off for ever. 11 In the day that thou stoodest on the other side, in the day that the strangers carried away captive his forces, and foreigners entered into his gates, and cast lots upon Jerusalem, even thou wast as one of them. 12 But thou shouldest not have looked on the day of thy brother in the day that he became a stranger; neither shouldest thou have rejoiced over the children of Judah in the day of their destruction; neither shouldest thou have spoken proudly in the day of distress. 13 Thou shouldest not have entered into the gate of my people in the day of their calamity; yea, thou shouldest not have looked on their affliction in the day of their calamity, nor have laid hands on their substance in the day of their calamity; 14 Neither shouldest thou have stood in the crossway, to cut off those of his that did escape; neither shouldest thou have delivered up those of his that did remain in the day of distress.

1.10-14 The violence you have dispensed now overwhelms you Edom. You drink of the cup you have served for generations. The sword you wielded will now execute you. God documents His verdict on Edom. Edom stood by and watched as his brother Jacob was attacked and bloodied. This points to our obligation to help our brother. This is illustrated in the New Testament by the parable of the Good Samaritan. Jesus asked the pointed question, "Who is my neighbor?" God set down a principal that if you refuse to help your brother when he is in need you are not absolved of guilt. The calamity of a brother reaches into our realm of responsibility. We are our brother's keeper.

1.15-16 For the day of the Lord is near upon all the heathen: as thou hast done, it shall be done unto thee: thy reward shall return upon thine own head. 16 For as ye have drunk upon my holy mountain, so shall all the heathen drink continually, yea, they shall drink, and they shall swallow down, and they shall be as though they had not been.

1.15-16 Divine retribution continues to be the pronounced edict of God on Edom. As you have done to others, so shall it be done to you. The day has come, judgment has arrived. Edom chose their reward by how they lived. This is the universal principal of God. Man chooses his judgment, God only pronounces it. You will drink what you have served others.

1.17-18 But upon mount Zion shall be deliverance, and there shall be holiness; and the house of Jacob shall possess their possessions. 18 And the house of Jacob shall be a fire, and the house of Joseph a flame, and the house of Esau for stubble, and they shall kindle in them, and devour them; and there shall not be any remaining of the house of Esau; for the Lord hath spoken it.

1.17-18 The promise of Jacob's triumph. After centuries of

letting the scales seem out of balance, God now reassures the world judgment will arrive in due time. It will flow from God's chosen people. Esau and all his offspring will eventually be usurped by Jacob and his offspring. Jacob will be a fire and Esau will be stubble, and none shall remain of the house of Esau.

1.19-21 And they of the south shall possess the mount of Esau; and they of the plain the Philistines: and they shall possess the fields of Ephraim, and the fields of Samaria: and Benjamin shall possess Gilead. 20 And the captivity of this host of the children of Israel shall possess that of the Canaanites, even unto Zarephath; and the captivity of Jerusalem, which is in Sepharad, shall possess the cities of the south. 21 And saviours shall come up on mount Zion to judge the mount of Esau; and the kingdom shall be the Lord's.

1.19-21 The spoil of war will be bequeathed upon Jacob's offspring. The final verdict is pronounced. Edom you are forever judged, Jacob you are forever blessed.

The Story Behind the Expository Series

This is a story about a man, his morals, and his ethics. The man's name was Millard Deramus. He was my paternal grandfather.

Millard lived at the end of a dirt and gravel road in Western Central Arkansas. When the road, as it was, reached his homestead, it turned and headed out of the woods. He was born a quarter of a mile from where he lived his entire life. I am not sure if he ever ventured out of the state of Arkansas. Possibly he got as far as a neighboring state once.

Many years ago he had a neighbor he simply referred to as Mr. Poole. One day Mr. Poole left. When it came time to pay the yearly taxes on their property, Mr. Poole had not returned. Millard was a good neighbor, so he did what he felt good neighbors do, he decided Mr. Poole's taxes should be paid so when Mr. Poole returned, he would not be in arrears with the state of Arkansas.

Millard hitched his mules and went on to Mr. Poole's land and cut a load of pulp wood and took it to the mill and sold it. He then went to the county seat and paid Mr. Poole's taxes. The next year Mr. Poole had still not returned, so Millard again cut pulp wood off Mr. Poole's land, sold it, and paid the taxes on Mr. Poole's land. This continued for many, many years. Mr. Poole never returned and each year my grandfather would cut timber off of Mr. Poole's land and sell it and pay the taxes on Mr. Poole's land.

I was there the day the attorney came to see Millard. We were on the back porch that had been screened in, and we were drinking coffee. I still have the two coffee cups we used that day. I heard the conversation from three feet away. The attorney had a briefcase full of papers he wanted Millard to sign.

The attorney informed Millard that according to the state of Arkansas, Millard was the owner of the 280 acres next door by the default of paying the taxes for the last 20 years. The name Millard Deramus was on every yearly receipt for over 20 years. The amount of money being discussed was substantial. I watched my grandfather closely. There was no reaction at all. No smile, not even a raised eyebrow.

Millard patiently waited for the attorney to finish. The attorney requested my grandfather sign the documents accepting ownership of 280 acres that joined his 70 acres. The value of the land at that time, including the timber, was well over a quarter of a million dollars. When the attorney finished and asked my grandfather to sign the documents he quietly and firmly said no, I will not sign. He informed the attorney that was not his land and he had never taken anything that did not belong to him in his life.

The amount of money was staggering to me. I was watching a man who had lived a simple rustic life for all of his eighty-plus years. He wore bib overalls and drove old pick-up trucks. When younger, he worked as a blacksmith out under the oak tree in his yard. I still have items he forged under that old oak tree. I watched that day as the attorney attempted to stoke the fire of avarice in Millard Deramus.

The attorney told Millard all he could do with several hundred thousand dollars. He floated the idea of a new home, a new truck, retirement, travel. Millard just stared at the attorney. No comment. None. The attorney tried again. Will you just sign, Millard? For your children? No comment. None. Finally the attorney asked, "Is there anything I can do to get you to sign these papers?" My grandfather simply shook his head no. He said one sentence. He said, "It ain't my land."

My grandfather died and was buried a short distance from where he lived his entire life. My grandmother (Dolly) lived a few more years. The children convinced her to sign the papers to claim ownership of the land because otherwise it would simply go back to the state. She signed, the land was sold, and my father was one of eight children who inherited.

When my father died I received my inheritance, part of which was the money from the sale of Mr. Poole's land. For a long time I pondered what to do. I did not feel like I could accept money I had witnessed my grandfather refuse on the afternoon on the back porch so many years before. So I waited. I did nothing. I never spent one dime of that money.

In 2016 an idea came to me that seemed an appropriate way to use that money. It is the money being used to produce the Expository Series. I did not know of any Apostolic writings that were doing an Expository Series. So I took that money and began to print books for Apostolic people to read.

The books of the Expository Series are printed without charge to the authors. The proceeds and profit of the books sold online go back into a non-profit fund to print more Apostolic books. None of the online profit is going to any personal use for anyone. If an author buys his book direct from wholesale after it is published and sells it, then he is welcomed to keep any profit from those sales.

I would like to thank all the men who have contributed their work to this endeavor. Scott Hall, Bart Adkins, Vaughn Reece, Kevin Archer, Ben Weeks, and Edward Seabrooks have all contributed. We have now published fifteen volumes and have three more to be published in the next sixty days. Others have also shown interest in publishing their works. Our goal is to have twenty volumes published by the end of 2017.

The publisher we are using has informed me we are their best seller they have ever published. We have now sold several thousand dollars of books since September 1, 2016. I am deeply grateful to everyone who has purchased our product.

Now you know the story behind the Expository Series. A simple Christian man with ethics and morals, opened his heart, and showed me his faith on a warm spring day, in a simple homestead, many years ago. Today I say thank you to my grandfather, Millard Deramus. Thank you for your ethics. Thank you for your morals. Thank you for your Christian faith.

May your memory be blessed and revered. You never

travelled 100 miles from where you were born, but your legacy has spanned America.

www.ingramcontent.com/pod-product-compliance
Lightning Source LLC
Chambersburg PA
CBHW040418100526
44588CB00022B/2869